Key Stage 2 LEARN

Grammar

NAPE
National Association for Primary Education

Contents

AUTHOR: Camilla de la Bédoyère
EDITORIAL: Catherine de la Bédoyère, Quentin de la Bédoyère, John Bolt, Vicky Garrard, Kate Lawson, Sally MacGill, Julia Rolf, Lyndall Willis
DESIGN: Jen Bishop, Dave Jones, Colin Rudderham
ILLUSTRATORS: David Benham, Sarah Wimperis
PRODUCTION: Chris Herbert, Claire Walker
Thanks also to Robert Walster

COMMISSIONING EDITOR: Polly Willis
PUBLISHER AND CREATIVE DIRECTOR: Nick Wells

3 Book Pack ISBN 1-84451-052-2   Book ISBN 1-84451-032-8
6 Book Pack ISBN 1-84451-066-2   Book ISBN 1-84451-079-4
First published in 2003

A copy of the CIP data for this book is available from the British Library upon request.

Created and produced by
FLAME TREE PUBLISHING
Crabtree Hall,
Crabtree Lane,
Fulham, London SW6 6TY
United Kingdom
www.flametreepublishing.com

Flame Tree Publishing is part of The Foundry Creative Media Co. Ltd.

© The Foundry Creative Media Co. Ltd, 2003

Printed in Croatia

Foreword

Sometimes when I am crossing the playground on my way to visit a primary school I pass young children playing at schools. There is always a stern authoritarian little teacher at the front laying down the law to the unruly group of children in the pretend class. This puzzles me a little because the school I am visiting is very far from being like the children's play. Where do they get this Victorian view of what school is like? Perhaps it's handed down from generation to generation through the genes. Certainly they don't get it from their primary school. Teachers today are more often found alongside their pupils, who are learning by actually doing things for themselves, rather than merely listening and obeying instructions.

Busy children, interested and involved in their classroom reflect what we know about how they learn. Of course they learn from teachers but most of all they learn from their experience of life and their life is spent both in and out of school. Indeed, if we compare the impact upon children of even the finest schools and teachers, we find that three or four times as great an impact is made by the reality of children's lives outside the school. That reality has the parent at the all important centre. No adult can have so much impact, for good or ill, as the young child's mother or father.

This book, and others in the series, are founded on the sure belief that the great majority of parents want to help their children grow and learn and that teachers are keen to support them. The days when parents were kept at arm's length from schools are long gone and over the years we have moved well beyond the white line painted on the playground across which no parent must pass without an appointment. Now parents move freely in and out of schools and very often are found in the classrooms backing up the teachers. Both sides of the partnership know how important it is that children should be challenged and stimulated both in and out of school.

Perhaps the most vital part of this book is where parents and children are encouraged to develop activities beyond those offered on the page. The more the children explore and use the ideas and techniques we want them to learn, the more they will make new knowledge of their very own. It's not just getting the right answer, it's growing as a person through gaining skill in action and not only in books. The best way to learn is to live.

I remember reading a story to a group of nine year old boys. The story was about soldiers and of course the boys, bloodthirsty as ever, were hanging on my every word. I came to the word khaki and I asked the group "What colour is khaki?" One boy was quick to answer. "Silver" he said, "It's silver." "Silver? I queried. "Yes," he said with absolute confidence, "silver, my Dad's car key is silver." Now I reckon I'm a pretty good teller of stories to children but when it came down to it, all my dramatic reading of a gripping story gave way immediately to the power of the boy's experience of life. That meant so much more to him, as it does to all children.

JOHN COE
General Secretary
National Association for Primary Education (NAPE).

NAPE was founded 23 years ago with the aim of improving the quality of teaching and learning in primary schools. The association brings together parents and teachers in partnership.

NAPE, Moulton College, Moulton, Northampton, NN3 7RR, Telephone: 01604 647 646 Web: www. nape.org.uk

Grammar is one of six books in the **Learn** series, which has been devised to help you support your child through Key Stage Two.

The book contains all the essential elements of good grammar and it can guide you, the parent, through part of the National Literacy Framework. This Framework identifies the need for children to learn reading and writing skills at three different levels; word, sentence and text. The balance between these levels is important; the Spelling book in the series should be studied in conjunction with Grammar. Daily reading, of both fiction and non-fiction, will further develop a sound understanding of texts and will contribute to the organisation and accuracy of a child's work.

Each page contains exercises for your child to complete, an activity they can complete away from book and Parents Start Here boxes to give you extra information and guidance. At the end of the book you will find a checklist of topics – you can use this to mark off each topic as it is mastered.

This book has been designed for children to work through alone; but it is recommended that you read the book first to acquaint yourself with the material it contains. **Try to be at hand when your child is working with the book; your input is valuable.**

Encourage good study habits in your child:

- Try to set aside a short time every day for studying. 10 to 20 minutes a day is plenty.

- Establish a quiet and comfortable environment for your child to work and suitable tools e.g. sharp pencils and good handwriting pens.

- Give your child access to drinking water whenever they work; research suggests this helps them perform better.

- Reward your child; plenty of praise for good work motivates children to succeed.

- Ensure your child eats a healthy diet, gets plenty of rest and lots of opportunity to play.

This book is intended to support your child in their school work. Sometimes children find particular topics hard to understand; discuss this with their teacher, who may be able to suggest alternative ways to help your child.

Top Tip! Go through this page as often as you like until your child understands it fully.

Parents Start Here ...

Organise your child to start their Word Book. We will be using it throughout this book.

Nouns

A noun is the name of a place, person or thing.

Common Nouns

These name places, people or things in general:

brother, country, town, apple, team.

Common nouns **start with** small letters.

Circle all of the common nouns in these sentences. The first one has been done for you.

a) My youngest brother really hates ice-cream and jelly. (3)

b) I climbed the mountain but my feet were very sore. (2)

c) Jenny's favourite lunch contains sandwiches, fruit and crisps. (4)

d) The bee flew to the flower and buzzed. (2)

Proper Nouns

These name particular places, people or things:

Tom, Wales, Glasgow, Cox, Arsenal.

Proper nouns **start with** capital letters.

Circle all of the proper nouns in these sentences. The first one has been done for you.

a) When Mabel visited Hampshire she took her dog, Spot.

b) I went to Chelsea to see my favourite rose, which is called Delightful.

c) My pal Sam lives in Richmond Avenue.

d) The twins are called George and Celia.

Collective Nouns

These name groups or collections of places, people or things:

swarm, pride, pack, pile, set, shoal.

Collective nouns start with small letters.

Choose the best words to complete the sentences.

a) A _____ of bees chased Harry down the road. (herd, flock, swarm)

b) Nelson and his _____ of ships saved the country. (flight, fleet, choir)

c) My Mum's stamp _____ is worth £500. (collection, team, packet)

d) The gorilla threw the _____ of bananas back at me. (forest, library, bunch)

Home Learn

Find the meanings of these collective nouns and write a sentence using each one. Use a dictionary to help you.

1. Shoal: _____   3. Host: _____

2. Clutch: _____   4. Pride: _____

Activity

Make a Word Book. Use an exercise or note book to record all the new words you learn. Put down the meanings of the words and check you have spelt them properly.

Check Your Progress!

Nouns

Turn to page 48 and put a tick next to what you have just learned.

Top Tip!
Bring what your child learns into everyday life – they'll remember it even better.

Parents Start Here ...

We will cover tenses, in more detail, later in the book.

Verbs

A verb is a word that usually describes an action.

You have probably been calling verbs 'doing words' until now.

Every sentence has a verb in it.

Verbs tell us what someone or something is doing or what is happening.

Some verbs are doing words, but some are being words.

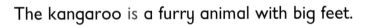

The kangaroo leaps over the bush.

This is a doing verb. It tells us what the kangaroo is doing.

The kangaroo is a furry animal with big feet.

This is a being verb. It tells us what the kangaroo is.

1. Circle the doing verb in these sentences. The first one has been done for you.

a) The big lion (roared) at the cub.

b) Starfish crawl along the sand.

c) Pirates steal treasure.

d) The planets move through space.

2. Choose a being verb to complete these sentences.

are   was   is   will be   were   am

a) Aliens _____ creatures that come from another planet.

b) King Alfred _____ the king who burned the cakes.

c) Next Tuesday I _____ one week older.

d) The Romans _____ good at building roads.

Verbs tell us when something happens:

I was thirsty.	(in the past)	Dogs barked.
I am thirsty.	(in the present)	Dogs bark.
I will be thirsty.	(in the future)	Dogs will bark.

Home Learn

Circle the doing verbs and underline the being verbs.

a) Tracy is mad, she hates chocolate.

b) The fat hippo waddled into the water so he could be cool.

c) The ship sailed away from the pirates, and it was safe.

d) Julius Caesar said "I came, I saw, I conquered". He was very boastful.

 ## Activity

Write the verb 'conquer' in to your Word Book. If you don't know its meaning, look it up in the dictionary. Can you think of a common noun that sounds the same as 'conquer'?

Check Your Progress!

Verbs ☐

Turn to page 48 and put a tick next to what you have just learned.

Top Tip! Don't worry if your child does not understand straightaway – children learn at different speeds.

Parents Start Here ...

Help your child discover interesting similes. Some of them could be recorded in the back of the Word Book.

Adjectives

An adjective is a word that describes a noun.

Adjectives give us more information about a place, person or thing.

Good adjectives can improve a sentence, and make it more interesting.

Sometimes adjectives are right next to the noun they are describing, but sometimes they are elsewhere in the sentence.

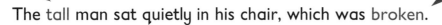

Adjectives can describe feelings.

Hairy monsters frighten me.

This is an adjective: it is describing monsters.

The tall man sat quietly in his chair, which was broken.

This is an adjective: it is describing the man.

This is also an adjective: it is describing the chair.

The pixie was upset when he heard the news.

This is an adjective: it is describing how the pixie was feeling.

8

Similes

Adjectives can also be used in similes.

A simile compares one thing to another.

Similes often use the words as or like.

I am as blind as a bat

simile

Your feet smell like cheese

simile

He was as cool as a cucumber

simile

Home Learn

Circle the adjectives.

a) The coalminer's face was black.

b) Nellie the Elephant was pleased when she saw the iced bun.

c) Puppies are cute.

d) When it rains the sky turns grey.

e) The bananas were brown, ripe and smelly.

Activity

Think of three similes. They may be ones you have come across before, or you could make up your own.

Check Your Progress!

Adjectives

Turn to page 48 and put a tick next to what you have just learned.

Top Tip!
If your child loses concentration here, let them take a break.

Parents Start Here ...

Encourage your child to use adverbs and adjectives in their written school work. Even if they miss them out on the first draft, it is fine for them to add improvements afterwards.

Adverbs

An adverb is a word that tells us more about a verb.

Adverbs tell us how something happens.

When adverbs tell us how something happens they often end in –ly.

The child cried loudly.

This adverb describes how the child cried.

Circle the best adverbs:

a) The maggot poked his head out of the apple (gingerly/punctually).

b) Dr Smith held the patient's hand (loudly/gently).

c) Maggie (quickly/slowly) jumped into the pool.

d) She ran (up/out) the stairs.

Adverbs can be very useful when we are describing how something was said.

"I don't like sweets" she said rudely.
"I don't like sweets" she said shyly.

"Give me your money" he said gruffly.
"Give me your money" he said gently.

Home Learn

Choose the best adverbs:

proudly heavily carefully lightly loudly hesitantly fairly

a) The children shouted _____.

b) Butterflies flap their wings _____.

c) Grandma dabbed her eyes _____.

d) He put his head round the door _____.

e) Polly picked up the broken glass _____.

Activity

When you read a book, look for some adverbs. If you come across any you particularly like, put them in your Word Book. **(Did you spot the adverb in that sentence?!)**

Check Your Progress!

Adverbs

Turn to page 48 and put a tick next to what you have just learned.

Top Tip!
Remember to give your child lots of praise – they'll work so much better.

Parents Start Here ...

Award your child marks for their work on these pages.
Add the total scores at the end.

Putting It Into Practice: Good Writing 1

You have learnt about nouns, verbs, adjectives and adverbs. Now you can put some of them to good use.

Remember these things:

Proper nouns must begin with capital letters.

Every sentence must have a verb.

Adjectives and adverbs make sentences more interesting.

Adjectives and adverbs give us more information about the things they are describing.

1. Draw a face in this box. It could be a real person, an imaginary person, a monster or an alien.

Write some adjectives to describe the face you have drawn. Try to think of at least two adjectives for each part of the face:

a) The eyes are ⟶ _____

b) The mouth is ⟶ _____

c) The hair is ⟶ _____

d) The nose is ⟶ _____

e) The skin is ⟶ _____

Give your child one mark for each different adjective they employ. ☐

2. Turn these adjectives into adverbs, by adding –ly

a) deep ⟶ _____

b) sweet ⟶ _____

c) glad ⟶ _____

Award one mark for each. ☐

Write a sentence using one of the adverbs you have made:

Award up to two marks. ☐

3. Turn these adjectives into adverbs by taking off the –e and adding –y

a) simple ⟶ _____

b) horrible ⟶ _____

c) terrible ⟶ _____

Award one mark for each. ☐

Write a sentence using one of the adverbs you have made:

Award up to two marks. ☐

4. Turn these adjectives into adverbs by taking off the –y and adding –ily

a) easy ⟶ _____

b) lazy ⟶ _____

c) lucky ⟶ _____

Award one mark for each. ☐

Write a sentence using one of the adverbs you have made:

Award up to two marks. ☐

Total marks. ☐

20+ marks ✻✻✻ Excellent!
10-19 marks ✻✻ Well done!
0-9 marks ✻ Great effort!

Check Your Progress!
Good Writing 1 ☐

Turn to page 48 and put a tick next to what you have just learned.

Top Tip!
If your child struggles with anything, don't worry – let them go at their own pace.

Parents Start Here ...

Your child will have covered these punctuation marks in Key Stage One. However, it is prudent to ensure they are competent at using them before progressing any further.

Punctuation

Punctuation marks make writing easier to understand.

Full stops mark the end of sentences.

Some sentences are short.

Some sentences can go on and on without ever taking a break and it gets quite hard to keep reading them out loud because you run out of breath. Phew!

Good punctuation means using full stops wisely.

Capital Letters are used at the beginning of sentences.

Capital letters are also used at the beginning of proper nouns:

My sister, Carrie, loves watching Star Wars. Do you?

Commas are used to mark pauses in sentences:

Max had to carry his bike, even though he had a bad shoulder, all the way home.

Commas are also used to separate lists of words:

Gemma made a fruit salad with bananas, apples, pears and oranges.

If you are not sure where to put a comma, just read the sentence out loud and listen for the natural breaks. They are usually good places to put commas.

Put the capital letters, commas and full stops into these sentences:

a) the stars were shining brightly

b) my favourite planet is venus it is the brightest planet I've seen

c) when the wind blows the waves swirl the gulls squawk and brighton becomes a wild place

Home Learn

Rewrite these sentences and put in the correct punctuation:

a) in my pencil case pens pencils rubbers and I keep

_____

b) bat ball and pads I can't play cricket my without

_____

c) around the world we sailed africa asia america visiting and

_____

d) of punctuation types commas full stops and capital letters are all

_____

 ## Activity

Write your own jumbled sentences and see if a friend can put them into a sensible order and add the correct punctuation.

Check Your Progress!
Punctuation ☐
Turn to page 48 and put a tick next to what you have just learned.

Parents Start Here ...

When you help your child with written work, encourage them to use the new punctuation marks they have learnt.

Question Marks And Exclamation Marks

Question marks are used to mark the end of a sentence that contains a question.

How many lumps of sugar would you like?

Exclamation marks are used to mark the end of a sentence that shows the writer feels strongly about something.

I hate it when you shout at me!

Exclamation marks can be used to show surprise or excitement:

That's just what I've always wanted!

Exclamation marks can be used to give a warning:

Get out!

Exclamation marks are great fun to use – but don't be tempted to put them everywhere. They lose their power when they are scattered all over the page.

Look at these pictures and write down what you think each person might be saying. Remember to use exclamation or question marks.

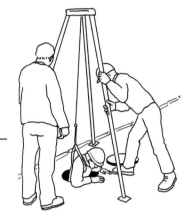

Home Learn

Punctuate each of these sentences:

a) please could I have a lemonade a burger and fries

b) get some help I'm hurt

c) why is your bedroom floor covered in junk

c) wait until your father gets home

Activity

Colour in the pictures above.

Check Your Progress!
Question Marks And Exclamation Marks

Turn to page 48 and put a tick next to what you have just learned.

Top Tip! Don't worry if your child does not understand straightaway – children learn at different speeds.

Parents Start Here ...

Help your child set out dialogue properly. Look at a fiction book if you get stuck.

Speech Marks

Speech marks are used to show direct speech.

When we write the exact words that someone has said, we call this direct speech.

We put speech marks, or inverted commas, to show the exact words that were spoken.

Speech marks, or inverted commas, look like this: " "

The speech marks at the beginning of the spoken words look like the number 66 : "

The speech marks at the end of the spoken words look like the

Number 99: "

A conversation is called a dialogue.

"Could you tell me how much that costs?" asked Timmy.

"Do you mean the one with orange stripes?" queried Mr Bloggs.

"No," replied Timmy "I'm interested in the one with red spots."

"Ah, well that's £2.99" said Mr Bloggs, with a smile.

Look at this dialogue and you will notice a VERY IMPORTANT THING. The punctuation that goes with the speech stays inside the speech marks.

Put a tick next to the sentences that have been correctly punctuated:

"Do you want to come with me"? she asked. ☐

"Do you want to come with me?" she asked. ☐

The policeman yelled "get off that roof!" as he chased the boys. ☐

The policeman yelled "get off that roof"! as he chased the boys. ☐

"Yes", said Milly. "I'd like that very much". ☐

"Yes," said Milly "I'd like that very much." ☐

Home Learn

Write your own direct speech to complete these sentences. You might need to add some punctuation.

a)   The nurse asked "_____"

"_____" replied the child.

b)   The teacher shouted "_____"

"_____" the boy shouted back.

c)   "_____" Mum asked me.

"_____" I said.

Activity

TRY THIS

Listen to a conversation, at school, the shops or at home. Try and write it out in the form of direct speech. Start a new line whenever another person starts talking.

Check Your Progress!
Speech Marks ☐
Turn to page 48 and put a tick next to what you have just learned.

Top Tip!
Go through this page as often as you like until your child understands it fully.

Parents Start Here ...

Some children get extremely confused by this subject so take it slowly. Putting apostrophes of possession into plural forms will be covered later.

Apostrophes

Apostrophes are used to show possession.

This means that something belongs to someone.

My cat's name is Tabitha.

The name of my cat is Tabitha.

Tabitha's fur is stripy.

The fur of Tabitha is stripy.

Write these sentences using apostrophes to show possession. The first one has been done for you.

a) The coat of Mr Black has a purple lining.

   Mr Black's coat has a purple lining.

b) The belly of the hippo was big.

   _____

c) The trousers of Edmund were full of holes.

   _____

d) One of the eyes of the goldfish was swollen.

   _____

Apostrophes are also used to show that one or more letters is missing.

Tabitha's a very lively cat.

the apostrophe replaces i. If the missing letter is put back sentence would say Tabitha is a very lively cat.

When words are shortened like this we call them contractions.

Here are some examples:

it is ➡ it's   we are ➡ we're   you are ➡ you're

we will ➡ we'll   who is ➡ who's   you have ➡ you've

I would ➡ I'd   are not ➡ aren't   do not ➡ don't

Home Learn

Copy each sentence, writing out the contracted words in full:

a) Next time we'll go swimming.

_____

b) Who's going to be my partner?

_____

c) Don't tell me you've done it again!

_____

d) We're going to the play.

_____

Activity

Practise writing out the contractions and make sure you've put the apostrophes in the correct place.

Check Your Progress!
Apostrophes

Turn to page 48 and put a tick next to what you have just learned.

Parents Start Here ...

Reading is the best way to get a feel for when a new paragraph is warranted. Continue to read regularly with your child, taking it in turns to read aloud.

Phrases, Sentences And Paragraphs

A sentence is a group or collection of words that makes sense.

- A sentence must contain a verb.
- A sentence starts with a capital letter and ends with a punctuation mark, such as a full stop, exclamation mark or question mark.

The unicorn galloped through the woods, chasing a rainbow.

This is a sentence.

A phrase is a group or collection of words that do not make sense on their own.

A phrase does not necessarily contain a verb and most phrases are short.

through the woods

This is a phrase. It doesn't have a verb and it doesn't make sense.

The phrases have been underlined:

The whale dived <u>through the waves</u>.

He opened his present, throwing paper <u>across the room</u>.

The ball bounced three times, then disappeared <u>over the wall</u>.

A paragraph is a group or collection of sentences that cover one subject.

The beginning of a paragraph is marked by a space between lines, or an indentation.

Look at a book or a newspaper to find how the beginning and ends of paragraphs are marked.

ANCIENT CALENDARS   25

In the second century AD, Ptolemy lived and studied in Alexandria. His famous summaries of Greek astronomical ideas and his theories of the universe dominated western ideas on astronomy until the time of Copernicus. He placed earth at the centre of the universe, with the planets revolving around it. Behind him is the goddess Astronomia.

ORIGINS OF THE MODERN CALENDAR
THE HISTORY of humankind's measurements of days, months and years is the history of civilisation and, it has been argued, its titanic conflict between sacred and secular political forces. It has propelled us through a history of ideas and understanding to a point at the start of the third millennium where we can measure the beginnings of the universe itself, rather than just rely on articles of faith, myth or simple conjecture.

The Ancient World, with its immense reserves of learning stretching from the ancient Chinese to the Greeks, Babylonians and Vedic Indians, struggled to explain the rhythm of the year using mathematical and astronomical observations that were, by the end of the first millennium, the envy of an embarrassed Europe cloaked in the Dark Ages. The balance of knowledge then shifted, with ideas and learning flooding through Europe, resulting in the powerful cultural synthesis of the Renaissance and ultimately causing the separation of sacred and secular authority over the instruments of time. This is significant

Home Learn

Tick the sentences:

a) My old man's a dustman.

b) A dustman's hat

c) The round table

d) King Arthur and his knights fought the war.

e) Big Brother

f) Big Brother is watching you.

Activity

Listen to the lyrics (words) of your favourite songs. You'll notice that sometimes the singer sings whole sentences, but sometimes they just use phrases.

Check Your Progress!
Phrases, Sentences and Paragraphs
Turn to page 48 and put a tick next to what you have just learned.

Top Tip! If your child loses concentration here, let them take a break.

Parents Start Here ...

When your child has finished writing their story, you can award them the following extra marks:

1 mark for using capital letters, full stops and commas.
3 marks if they were always used correctly.
2 marks for using paragraphs.
1–3 marks for handwriting and presentation.

Putting It Into Practice: Good Writing 2

Continue this story. Don't worry about the ending, or even the plot. Just describe the graveyard, the two boys and how they are feeling. Include some dialogue between the boys that might explain why they are there. Think about what you are going to write, before you start.

It was late in the evening and a dappled, silvery light settled on to the gravestones. Harry and George shivered slightly, even though the heat from the day still hung heavily around them.

_____

_____

_____

_____

_____

How many adjectives did you use? ☐

3 + = 3 marks
1–2 = 1 mark

Write your best adjective here:

_____

How many adverbs did you use? ☐

> 3 + = 3 marks
> 1–2 = 1 mark

Write your best adverb here:

_____

Check your dialogue. Have you used your speech marks correctly? Yes/No.

If not, make your corrections.

_____

_____

_____

_____

_____

Total marks. ☐

20+ marks   ✷ ✷ ✷ Excellent!
10-19 marks   ✷ ✷ Well done!
0-9 marks   ✷ Great effort!

Check Your Progress!
Good Writing 2 ☐

Turn to page 48 and put a tick next to
what you have just learned.

Top Tip!
If your child struggles with anything, don't worry – let them go at their own pace.

Parents Start Here ...

Possessive pronouns are often confused with some contractions (it's/ its, who's/whose) or other words that sound the same (their/there).

Pronouns

A pronoun is a word that takes the place of a noun.

The man shook his umbrella.

He shook his umbrella

He has taken the place of the man.

These are all pronouns:

you   we   he   she   it   I   them

Replace the highlighted words with suitable pronouns:

a) When the mouse began to run, the cat chased the mouse _____.

b) I asked Dan to give me a lolly but Dan _____ said he'd eaten all of the lollies _____.

c) When Sally and I went to the park Sally and I _____ had a big argument.

Using pronouns sounds much better, doesn't it?

Possessive pronouns are pronouns that tell us when something is owned by someone.

Possessive pronouns never have an apostrophe.

These are all possessive pronouns:

Yours   ours   his   your   hers   its   my   their   theirs   whose

Jerry's coat   ➡   his coat

Carole's story   ➡   her story

Jack and Jill's journey   ➡   their journey

> Look at the possessive pronoun its and remember this:
> Its never has an apostrophe unless it is short for it is.
> You won't believe how many grown-ups get this wrong, but it is
> a simple rule and there is no excuse for making this lazy mistake.

Home Learn

Use it's or its to complete the sentence

a) _____ a lovely day today.

b) The dog wagged _____ tail.

c) My mother said _____ too late to go out now.

d) When _____ dark the ghosts come out.

e) A crocodile loses _____ teeth occasionally.

f) The horse lost _____ footing and fell over.

g) _____ never too late to learn good grammar.

Activity

Look out for its and it's being written incorrectly. You can even
find it occurring in newspapers, magazines and books!

> **Check Your Progress!**
>   **Pronouns** ☐
> Turn to page 48 and put a tick next to what you have just learned.

Top Tip!
Remember to give your child lots of praise – they'll work so much better.

Parents Start Here ...

Learning terms such as preposition and conjunction, and becoming familiar with their use, will help your child master foreign languages.

Prepositions

Prepositions are words that show the position of one thing in relation to another.

The cow jumped over the moon.

This word tells us the position of the cow to the moon.

These are all prepositions:

over   across   at   by   on   up   with   down   into   off
before   under   above   beside   between   behind   in

Ring the prepositions:

Under the bramble

Beside the tree

My true love's waiting,

Weeping for me.

Far across the waves

Over the sea,

I know she's waiting

Near the plum tree.

Read this sentence and underline the prepositions:

The snow fell on the pavement, its flakes scattered across the car roofs. Trickles of icy water ran over the edge of the kerb and down the drain. Above the grey clouds even darker clouds rolled, with the promise of more snow to come.

Home Learn

Put the missing prepositions into these sentences:

in   over   below   through

a) The horse jumped _____ the fence.

b) The clown threw the clubs _____ the air.

c) Billy crawled _____ the tunnel.

d) The owl looked at the ground _____ him.

Activity

Look in a fiction book and find three prepositions.

Check Your Progress!
Prepositions
Turn to page 48 and put a tick next to what you have just learned.

Parents Start Here ...

Your child has been asked to recall some of the things they learnt earlier in the book. Encourage them to dip back into the book to remind themselves of things they have forgotten.

Conjunctions

Conjunctions are words that join one sentence to another.

Mr Patel and Mrs Amit both went to the school meeting. They went in the same car.

Mr Patel and Mrs Amit both went to the school meeting so they went in the same car.

This conjunction made one sentence out of two sentences.

When a conjunction joins two sentences together the new sentence is called a compound sentence.

These are all conjunctions:

because   so   and   but   if   until   while   before   unless
after   although   since   though   when   where

Circle the conjunctions:

I went to bed early because I was so tired. I like to read in bed, unless I have just finished a book. I might watch television in bed but I didn't last night. I put my glasses on to read though I don't always need them. I opened my book and felt my eyelids close. I'd have stayed asleep if the cat hadn't startled me.

Write one possessive pronoun from the text: _____

Write one doing verb from the text: _____

Write one being verb from the text: _____

Write one pronoun from the text: _____

Write one preposition from the text: _____

Home Learn

Write three sentences using conjunctions:

1. _____

2. _____

3. _____

TRY THIS

Activity

Challenge a grown up or friend to identify the conjunctions in the sentences you have written.

Check Your Progress!

Conjunctions ☐

Turn to page 48 and put a tick next to what you have just learned.

Top Tip! Don't worry if your child does not understand straightaway – children learn at different speeds.

Parents Start Here ...

Children who use sophisticated parts of speech, such as superlatives and comparatives, in their work will be rewarded with good marks in National Tests.

Adjectives: Comparatives And Superlatives

An adjective is a word that describes a noun.

The Irish Sea is big.

Big is an adjective; it is describing the Irish Sea.

Comparative and superlative adjectives describe nouns in relation to one another.

A comparative is used to compare two nouns.

The Red Sea is bigger than the Irish Sea.

A comparative adjective

Comparatives often end in –er.

A superlative is used to compare three or more nouns.

The Mediterranean Sea is the biggest.

A superlative adjective

Superlative adjectives often end in –est.

Fill in the missing adjectives:

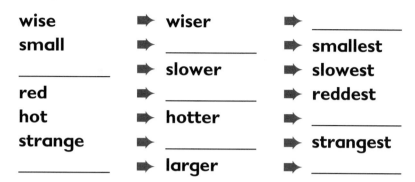

wise	➡ wiser	➡ _____
small	➡ _____	➡ smallest
_____	➡ slower	➡ slowest
red	➡ _____	➡ reddest
hot	➡ hotter	➡ _____
strange	➡ _____	➡ strangest
_____	➡ larger	➡ _____

Look again at red and hot. Can you say something about what you had to do to the adjective to make it into a comparative or a superlative?

Sometimes it might sound odd to put –er or –est on to the end of an adjective:

Which girl is intelligentest?   That sounds very peculiar.

In these cases we use more or most instead.

Which girl is most intelligent?   That sounds better.

Home Learn

To change these adjectives you need to take off the –y and add –ier or –iest. Complete the sentences using the adjectives you are given.

a) The second mouse was much _____(noisy) than the first.

b) My brothers are the _____ (lucky) people in their school.

c) Cinderella was _____ (pretty) than either of her step-sisters.

d) My grandparents are the _____(happy) people I know.

Activity

Think of three other adjectives that you can turn into comparatives and superlatives. Put them into your Word Book, with their superlative and comparative forms.

Check Your Progress!
Comparatives And Superlatives
Turn to page 48 and put a tick next to what you have just learned.

Top Tip! Bring what your child learns into everyday life – they'll remember it even better.

Parents Start Here ...

Go through this subject again with your child to reinforce it; this can be a difficult subject to grasp.

Spelling Plurals

Plural means more than one.

Singular is a word that means only one.

The simplest way to show a plural is to add –s.

cats   dogs   cars   telephones   cushions

The letter s is added to a singular word to show there is more than one.

Words that end in –ful also form a plural by adding –s.

cupful   ⟶   cupfuls

spoonful   ⟶   spoonfuls

boxful   ⟶   boxfuls

Words that end in –consonant + y form plurals by losing the –y and adding –ies.

baby   ⟶   babies

factory   ⟶   factories

There are some words that only exist in the plural form:

trousers   spectacles   tongs   pliers   measles   tweezers

Can you think of any others?

There are some words that are the same when they are singular or plural:

sheep   cod   dozen   trout   deer   innings

To use an apostrophe that shows possession for a plural word, put the apostrophe after the –s.

The plane's wings have fallen off.

The noun, plane, is singular, so just add –s.

All of the planes' wings have fallen off.

The noun, planes, is plural so put the apostrophe after it.

Home Learn

Put the correct singular/plural form in to these sentences:

a) I saw three red _____ .(lorry)

b) I've got three _____ of manure. (bucketful)

c) The traitor was hung from the _____ until he was dead. (gallows)

Put the apostrophe in the correct place:

d) The two boys jumpers are lost.

e) Two of the dogs feet were bleeding.

f) My aunts shoe is missing.

TRY THIS   Activity

Practise putting apostrophes of possession on to plurals – it can be confusing.

Check Your Progress!
Spelling Plurals
Turn to page 48 and put a tick next to what you have just learned.

Parents Start Here ...

Award one mark for each tick. Award an extra mark for each adjective or adverb your child uses (without being prompted to use them).

Putting It Into Practice: Good Writing 3

Your space rocket has landed on Planet Mungo. The locals don't seem too friendly, but you have a mission to collect Mungo Matter – a spongy substance that grows on the planet – and return it to Earth. (Scientists are hoping Mungo Matter will cure the Common Cold.)

Describe what the planet is like, and its inhabitants (the creatures who live there). Describe how you find the Mungo Matter and get it back to your rocket.

Be sure to use each of these at least once. Tick them off as you use them:

Speech marks ☐

A superlative ☐

A plural that ends in –s ☐

A conjunction ☐

A preposition ☐

A comparative ☐

A question mark ☐

An exclamation mark ☐

WELCOME TO MUNGO

_____

_____

_____

_____

_____

_____

_____

_____

_____

_____

Total marks. ☐

20+ marks ✳ ✳ ✳ Excellent!
10-19 marks ✳ ✳ Well done!
0-9 marks ✳ Great effort!

Check Your Progress! ☐
Good Writing 3
Turn to page 48 and put a tick next to
what you have just learned.

Parents Start Here ...

The selective use of similes and metaphors in the National Tests will earn your child extra marks. It also makes their work more interesting for the reader.

Idioms, Similes And Metaphors

Idioms are everyday expressions.

Idioms make speech or written work more interesting and lively.

> "In for a penny, in for a pound" said Granny as she climbed onto the rollercoaster. Granny may have been over the hill, but she still loved an adventure.

When idioms are used too often they become clichés.

Here are some other idioms you may be familiar with:

> Feeling under the weather
>
> Beat about the bush
>
> At the end of the day
>
> Bottom of my heart

> Idioms can make written work more interesting – but it is best not to use more than one in any written piece of work you do.

Similes compare one thing to another.

> We looked at some similes when we learnt about adjectives.
>
> Similes often use the words as or like.

As quiet as a mouse

The flower was blue, like the sky on a summer's day.

> Similes are a very useful way of spicing up your descriptions of people, places or things.

Metaphors are used to say one thing is another.

Metaphors give meaning to something, but are not literally true.

Metaphors are more powerful than similes.

The King raged with anger until the whole palace shook.

The palace did not really shake, but this shows you how very angry the king must have been.

Home Learn

Underline the similes in these sentences:

a) The sea tossed the ship from side to side, like a baby in a cradle.

b) Stevie hit the ball with such force it looked like a rocket destined for outer space.

c) The apple was as juicy as a freshly picked orange.

Activity

Write a list of five metaphors. Look out for similes and metaphors in your reading book.

Check Your Progress!
Idioms, Similes and Metaphors
Turn to page 48 and put a tick next to what you have just learned.

Parents Start Here ...

Ensure your child realises that the subject of a sentence is not necessarily the first noun in that sentence.

More About Sentences

Tenses

The tense of a verb tells us when something happened.

The future tense tells us about something that will happen:

I shall wait for a bus

I will wait for a bus

The present tense tells us about something happening right now:

I am waiting for a bus

I wait for a bus

The past tense tells us about something that has already happened:

I waited for a bus

I have waited for a bus

Subjects And Objects

Every simple sentence can be split into two parts: a subject and a predicate.

The subject of a sentence is the main person or thing.

The predicate of a sentence is everything else.

The predicate has the verb and it tells us what is happening.

The octopus grabbed the fish.

subject   predicate

Sentences usually have an object too.

The object of a sentence is the person or thing that is having something done to it.

The octopus grabbed the fish.

object

Home Learn

Ring the objects and underline the subjects:

a) The apple fell on to his head.

b) Two dolphins swam towards the coast.

c) I dropped the bread.

d) A dozen eggs were laid by one chicken!

e) The pop star sang his song beautifully.

Activity

Try to think of some sentences that do not have objects.

Check Your Progress!
More About Sentences
Turn to page 48 and put a tick next to what you have just learned.

Top Tip!
Learning is fun, so if your child is tired, let them come back to this when they are fresh.

Parents Start Here ...

Award up to 5 marks for presentation, up to 5 marks for content and up to 5 marks for punctuation.

Putting It Into Practice: Good Writing 4

Fiction

This describes stories that have been made up.

Non-Fiction

This describes stories that are true, or written work that is based on facts.

Write a non-fiction account.

Choose one of these titles:

The Worst Day Of My Life   **My Favourite Pastime**

My Family   **The Place Where I Live**

Plan the account first. Jot a quick sentence down that summarises what you will be talking about in each part of your account.

The beginning: _____

The middle: _____

The end: _____

Think about how you can make the account interesting and informative. Can you use some of the punctuation tools you have learnt about in this book?

_____

_____

_____

_____

_____

_____

_____

_____

_____

_____

_____

_____

_____

_____

_____

_____

Total marks. ☐

20+ marks   ✳ ✳ ✳ Excellent!
10-19 marks   ✳ ✳ Well done!
0-9 marks   ✳ Great effort!

Check Your Progress! ☐
Good Writing 4
Turn to page 48 and put a tick next to what you have just learned.

Parents Start Here ...

Award up to 5 marks for presentation, up to 5 marks for content and up to 5 marks for punctuation.

Putting It Into Practice: Good Writing 5

Write a fictional story.

Choose one of these titles:

Pooch the Pizza Thief

Adventure at Sea

The Incredible Shrinking Car

Three Girls and a Magic Mouse

Plan the story first.

Who are the main characters?

1. _____

2. _____

3. _____

What is the basic plot of the story? (what happens?)

_____

_____

Jot a quick sentence down that summarises what will be happening in each part of the story.

The beginning: _____

The middle: _____

The end: _____

Remember to use adjectives, adverbs, speech, similes or metaphors and perfect punctuation. Even though you will be concentrating hard on what you are writing you must try to keep your handwriting neat.

_____

_____

_____

_____

_____

_____

_____

_____

_____

_____

_____

Total marks. ☐

20+ marks   ✳ ✳ ✳ Excellent!
10-19 marks   ✳ ✳ Well done!
0-9 marks   ✳ Great effort!

Check Your Progress!
Good Writing 5 ☐

Turn to page 48 and put a tick next to what you have just learned.

Word Search

a	d	j	e	c	t	i	v	e	s	r	j	y	o
d	w	s	x	q	u	i	n	o	u	n	s	c	p
v	q	p	e	u	e	v	e	r	b	s	n	r	l
e	q	a	g	e	k	o	l	o	j	e	b	c	u
r	c	c	t	s	t	b	n	m	e	i	e	o	r
b	s	e	a	t	e	j	g	p	c	o	m	m	a
s	t	o	p	i	j	e	w	a	t	t	i	m	l
q	d	r	d	o	k	c	n	i	r	o	s	o	s
p	x	p	u	n	c	t	u	a	t	i	o	n	i
s	p	e	e	c	h	m	a	r	k	s	y	i	e

adjectives	adverbs	comma
common	nouns	object
plurals	punctuation	question
space	speech marks	stop
subject	verbs	

Answers

Pages 4–5
Common nouns:
b) mountain, feet
c) lunch, sandwiches, fruit, crisps
d) bee, flower
Proper nouns:
b) I, Chelsea, Delightful
c) Sam, Richmond Avenue
d) George, Celia
Collective nouns:
a) A swarm of bees chased Harry down the road.
b) Nelson and his fleet of ships saved the country.
c) My Mum's stamp collection is worth £500.
d) The gorilla threw the bunch of bananas back at me.

Pages 6–7
Verbs:
1. b) crawl
   c) steal
   d) move

2. a) Aliens are creatures that come from another planet.
   b) King Alfred was the king who burned the cakes.
   c) Next Tuesday I will be one week older.
   d) The Romans were good at building roads.

Home Learn
a) is = being verb
   hates = doing verb
b) waddled = doing verb
   could be = being verb
c) sailed = doing verb
   was = being verb
d) said, came, saw, conquered = doing verbs
   was = being verb

Page 9
Home Learn
a) black
b) pleased, iced
c) cute
d) grey
e) brown, ripe, smelly

Pages 10–11
Adverbs:
a) The maggot poked his head out of the apple gingerly.
b) Dr Smith held the patient's hand gently.
c) Maggie quickly jumped into the pool.
d) She ran up the stairs.

Home Learn
a) The children shouted loudly.
b) Butterflies flap their wings lightly.
c) Grandma dabbed her eyes proudly.
d) He put his head round the door hesitantly.
e) Polly picked up the broken glass carefully.

Pages 12–13
2. a) deeply
   b) sweetly
   c) gladly

3. a) simply
   b) horribly
   c) terribly

4. a) easily
   b) lazily
   c) luckily

Pages 14–15
Punctuation:
a) The stars were shining brightly.
b) My favourite planet is Venus. It is the brightest planet I've seen.
c) When the wind blows the waves swirl, the gulls squawk and Brighton becomes a wild place.

Home Learn
a) In my pencil case I keep pens, pencils, and rubbers.
b) I can't play cricket without my bat, ball and pads.
c) We sailed around the world visiting Africa, Asia and America.
d) Full stops, commas and capital letters are all types of punctuation.

Pages 17
Home Learn
a) Please could I have a lemonade, a burger and fries?
b) Get some help! I'm hurt.
c) Why is your bedroom floor covered in junk?
c) Wait until your father gets home!

Pages 18–19
Speech Marks:
"Do you want to come with me?" she asked.
The policeman yelled "get off that roof!" as he chased the boys.
"Yes," said Milly "I'd like that very much."

Pages 20–21
Apostrophes:
b) The hippo's belly was big.
c) Edmund's trousers were full of holes.
d) One of the goldfish's eyes was swollen.

Home Learn
a) Next time we will go swimming.
b) Who is going to be my partner?
c) Do not tell me you've done it again!
d) We are going to the play.

Page 23
Home Learn
The sentences are:
a) My old man's a dustman.
d) King Arthur and his knights fought the war.
f) Big Brother is watching you.

Pages 26–27
Pronouns:
a) When the mouse began to run the cat chased it.
b) I asked Dan to give me a lolly but he said he'd eaten all of them.
c) When Sally and I went to the park we had a big argument.

Home Learn
a) It's a lovely day today.
b) The dog wagged its tail.
c) My mother said it's too late to go out now.
d) When it's dark the ghosts come out.
e) A crocodile loses its teeth occasionally.
f) The horse lost its footing and fell over.
g) It's never too late to learn good grammar.

Pages 28–29
Prepositions:
Under
Beside
Across
Over
Near

The snow fell on the pavement, its flakes scattered across the car roofs. Trickles of icy water ran over the edge of the kerb and down the drain. Above the grey clouds even darker clouds rolled, with the promise of more snow to come.

Home Learn
a) The horse jumped over the fence.
b) The clown threw the clubs in the air.
c) Billy crawled through the tunnel
d) The owl looked at the ground below him.

Pages 30–31
Conjunctions:
I went to bed early because I was so tired. I like to read in bed, unless I have just finished a book. I might watch television in bed but I didn't last night. I put my glasses on to read though I don't always need them. I opened my book and felt my eyelids close. I'd have stayed asleep if the cat hadn't startled me.

Pages 32–33
Adjectives:

wise	wiser	wisest
small	smaller	smallest
slow	slower	slowest
red	redder	reddest
hot	hotter	hottest
strange	stranger	strangest
large	larger	largest

Home Learn
a) The second mouse was much noisier than the first.
b) My brothers are the luckiest people in their school.
c) Cinderella was prettier than either of her step-sisters.
d) My grandparents are the happiest people I know.

Page 35
Home Learn
a) I saw three red lorries.
b) I've got three bucketfuls of manure.
c) The traitor was hung from the gallows until he was dead.

Put the apostrophe in the correct place:
d) The two boys' jumpers are lost.
e) Two of the dog's feet were bleeding.
f) My aunt's shoe is missing.

Page 39
Home Learn
a) like a baby in a cradle.
b) like a rocket destined for outer space.
c) as juicy as a freshly picked orange.

Page 41
Home Learn
a) The apple fell on to his head.
b) Two dolphins swam towards the coast.
c) I dropped the bread.
d) A dozen eggs were laid by one chicken!
e) The pop star sang his song beautifully.

Page 46

Check Your Progress!

Nouns .... ☐

Verbs .... ☐

Adjectives .... ☐

Adverbs .... ☐

Good Writing 1 .... ☐

Punctuation .... ☐

Question Marks and Exclamation Marks .... ☐

Speech Marks .... ☐

Apostrophes .... ☐

Phrases, Sentences and Paragraphs .... ☐

Good Writing 2 .... ☐

Pronouns .... ☐

Prepositions .... ☐

Conjunctions .... ☐

Adjectives: Comparatives and Superlatives.................... ☐

Spelling Plurals... ☐

Good Writing 3 .... ☐

Idioms, Similes and Metaphors .... ☐

More about Sentences .... ☐

Good Writing 4 .... ☐

Good Writing 5 .... ☐